Camilla Gry
Favorite

String Games

Illustrated by Tom Sankey

SCHOLASTIC INC.

New York Toronto London Auckland Sydney
Mexico City New Delhi Hong Kong Buenos Aires

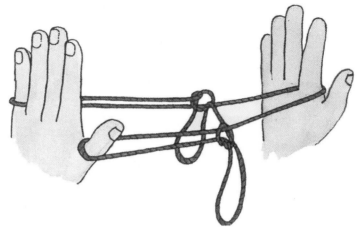

ISBN 0-439-77939-1

12 11 10 9 8 7 6 5 4 3   5 6 7 8 9 10/0

Printed in the U.S.A.   40

First Scholastic printing, June 2005

The material in this book originally appeared in *Cat's Cradle, Owl's Eyes*;
Many Stars and More String Games and *Super String Games*.

Chapter title string photograph by Steve Payne

Contents

Introduction

I've been walking around with a string in my pocket for 15 years now. It's just a simple loop of string, but I can weave it on my fingers to make intricate nets, butterflies, birds that fly and gates that open. I can do magic, play tricks on my friends and even tell stories with my string.

People from different cultures all over the world created string figures. There are Inuit string games, and there are string games from the South Pacific. String figures come from South America, Africa, China and Japan. In fact, there aren't many places in the world where people don't play with string.

We can learn string figures today because anthropologists collected them and wrote down the instructions using a special language. They recorded the stories and the traditions that went with the figures they learned from string artists.

I spend a lot of time with strings on my fingers, sharing string games and their stories — but that's only part of it. Wherever I go, I take hundreds of strings to give away, because I love to teach string figures as well.

The string games in this book are some of my very favorites, and they're the ones that people always want to learn. The patterns are beautiful, the magic is fun, and the way many of them move will surprise you. Start with the easier figures at the beginning of the book. After a little while, you'll get used to keeping the strings on your fingers and to the language I've used to tell you and your fingers what to do next. When you first learn a figure, you have to remember each step, but when you've made it a few times, your fingers will remember for you.

Have fun with the wonderful figures in this book — learn them, show them off and share them with your friends. And always carry a string in your pocket.

About the String

The Inuit used sinew or a leather thong to make their string figures. Other peoples farther south made twine from the inside of bark. We are told that Tikopian children in the Pacific Islands area preferred fiber from the hibiscus tree, although they would use a length of fishing line if it was handy. Some people even used human hair, finely braided.

Fortunately, you don't have to go out into the woods or cut your hair to get a good string for making string figures. You can use ordinary white butcher's string knotted together at the ends. Macrame cord also works quite well, since it is thicker than string. A thicker string loop will show off your string figures better.

Dressmaker's supply stores sell nylon cord, usually by the foot or meter. This kind of cord is probably the best, and because it is woven, not plied or twisted, it won't crease. It can be joined without a knot. A knot in your string loop can cause tangles, and figures that move won't go smoothly if there is a knot in the way.

How to Make Your String

You need about six feet (two meters) of string or cord, so that your string loop will measure three feet (one meter) when it is joined. This is a standard size. If this length seems uncomfortably long, a shorter string is fine for most of the figures.

The string can either be tied or melted together.

To tie your string

You need a knot that won't slip, so a square knot is best.

1 Lay the right end of the string across the left end.

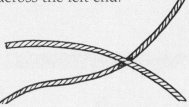

2 Put this right end under the left string to tie the first part of the knot.

3 Lay the new left end across the new right end.

4 Put this new left end under the new right string and tighten the knot.

5 Trim the ends to make the knot neat.

To melt your string

If the cord is nylon or some other synthetic fiber, you can melt the ends together. Joining the string takes practice, and it has to be done quickly, while the cord is hot. You will probably need some help, so please do this with an adult.

1 Hold the ends of the string near each other, about one-half inch (one to two centimeters) above a candle flame. If the ends are not melting at all, they are too far away from the flame. They will singe if you are holding them too close.

2 When the ends are gooey, stick them together.

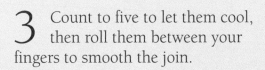

3 Count to five to let them cool, then roll them between your fingers to smooth the join.

You have now made your "play string," or "ayahaak," as the Inuit call it.

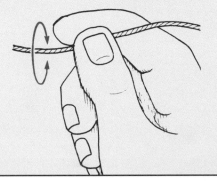

Terminology

There's a Special Language

A long time ago, people made lists of the names of string figures or brought back drawings of the finished patterns. Some even kept the string pattern itself, fastened to a piece of paper. But once a string figure is finished, it is almost impossible to tell just how it was made.

We can learn and teach each other string figures today because, in 1898, two anthropologists, Dr. A.C. Haddon and Dr. W.H.R. Rivers, invented a special language to describe the way string figures are made. Haddon and Rivers developed their special language to record all the steps it took to make the string figures they learned in the Torres Straits. Then, other anthropologists used this same language, or a simpler version of it, when they wanted to remember the string figures they saw in their travels.

The language used in this book to describe the making of the figures is similar to that used by Haddon and Rivers. The loops and the strings have names, and there are also names for some of the basic positions and moves.

About Loops

When the string goes around your finger or thumb, it makes a **loop.** The loops take their names from their location on your hands: **thumb loop, index loop, middle finger loop, ring finger loop, little finger loop.**

If you move a loop from one finger to another, it gets a new name: a loop that was on your thumb but is now on your little finger is a new little finger loop.

Each loop has a **near string** — the one nearer (or closer) to you — and a **far string** — the one farther from you.

If there are two loops on your thumb or finger, one is the **lower loop** — the one near the base of your thumb or finger — and the other is the **upper loop** — the one near the top of your thumb or finger. Don't get these loops mixed up, and be sure to keep them apart.

About Making the Figures

As you make the figures in this book, you will be weaving the strings of the loops on your fingers. Your fingers or thumbs can go over or under the strings to pick up one or more strings, then go back to the basic position.

Sometimes you may **drop** or **release** a loop from your fingers.

It takes a little while to get used to holding your hands so that the strings don't drop off your fingers. If you accidentally drop a loop or a string, it is best to start all over again.

Now go and get your string — let's begin!

NAMES OF THE STRINGS

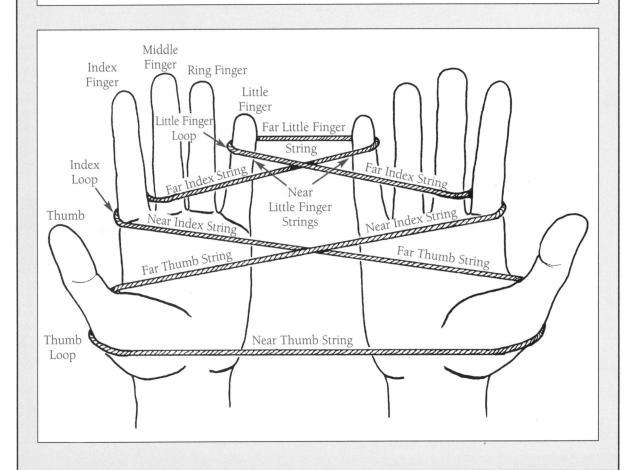

8

The Basic Position

Your hands begin in the **basic position** for most string figures and usually return to the basic position after each move.

1 Your hands are parallel, the palms are facing each other, and your fingers are pointing up.

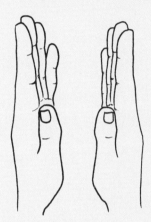

The hands in some of the pictures are not in the basic position. The hands are shown with the palms facing you so that you can see all the strings clearly.

Position 1

1 With your hands in the basic position, hang the loop of string on your thumbs. Stretch your hands as far apart as you can to make the string loop tight.

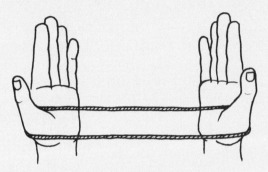

2 Pick up the far thumb string with your little fingers. The string that goes across the palm of your hand is called the **palmar string**.

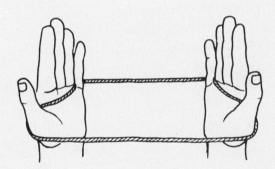

Opening A

Many string figures begin with **Opening A**.

1 Put the string loop on your fingers in Position 1.

2 With your right index finger, pick up, from below, the palmar string on your left hand and return to the basic position, pulling this string on the back of your index finger as far as it will go.

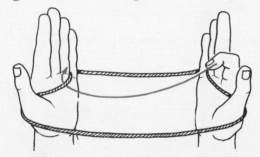

3 With your left index finger, pick up the right palmar string from below, in between the strings of the loop that goes around your right index finger. Return to the basic position, again pulling out the palmar string as far as it will go.

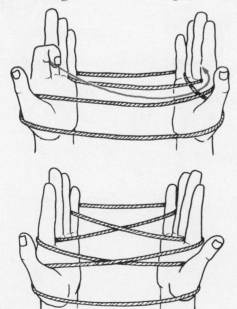

To Navaho a Loop

When you have two loops on your thumb or finger, a lower loop and an upper loop, you **Navaho** these loops by lifting the lower loop — with the thumb and index finger of your opposite hand, or with your teeth — up over the upper loop and over the tip of your finger or thumb.

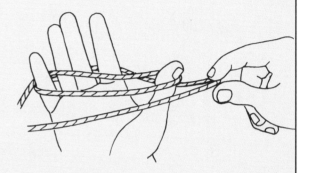

You can also Navaho a loop by tipping down your thumb or finger, letting the lower loop slip off, then straightening up your thumb or finger again.

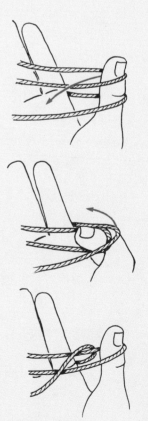

To Share a Loop

Sometimes you will **share a loop** between two fingers or a finger and your thumb. You use your opposite index finger and thumb to pull out the loop so that the other finger or thumb will fit into the loop as well.

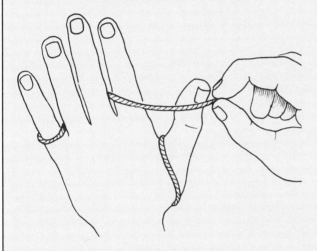

To Extend a Figure

Sometimes the strings may be woven and a figure may be finished, but it needs to be **extended** by pulling the hands apart or by turning or twisting the hands in a certain way. Extending the figure makes a tangle of strings magically turn into a beautiful pattern.

To Take the Figure Apart

Always take the figures apart gently — tugging creates knots. If the figure has top and bottom straight strings that frame the pattern, pull these apart and the pattern will dissolve.

Getting a String or Strings

When the instructions tell you to **get** a string or strings, your finger or thumb goes under that string, picks up that string on its back (the back of your finger or thumb is the side with the fingernail), then returns to the basic position, carrying the string with it. The instructions will tell you if you are to use your fingers or thumb to pick up the strings in a different way.

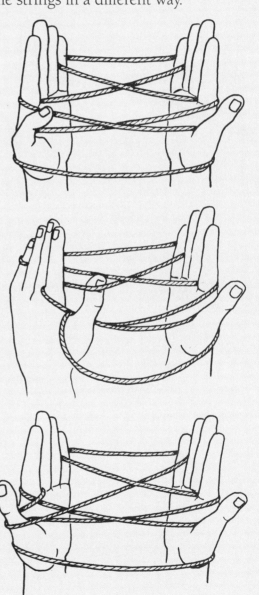

The Fish Spear

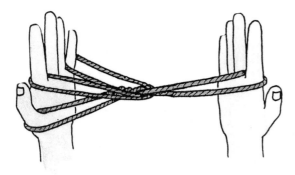

This string figure represented a fish spear or harpoon to the people who lived in the Torres Straits between Australia and New Guinea, a duck spear in Alaska, and a coconut palm tree in Africa. The Salish call it Pitching a Tent. You can call it a broom if you like.

1 Do Position 1.

2 Your right index finger goes under the left palmar string and pulls it out a little bit.

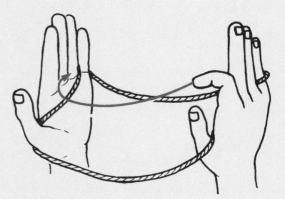

3 Your right index finger **twists its loop.** (See instructions below on how to twist a loop.)

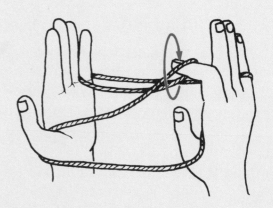

HOW TO TWIST A LOOP

Rotate your index finger away from you, down, towards you and up. Make sure the twist is in the string loop, not around your index finger.

Do it again. *There are now two twists in the strings of the right index loop.

4 Your right index finger pulls out its twisted loop as far as it will go.

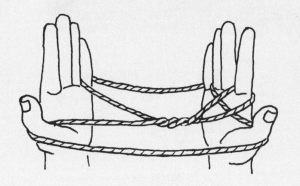

5 Your left index finger picks up, from below, the right palmar string between the strings of the right index loop. Now pull this loop out as far as it will go.

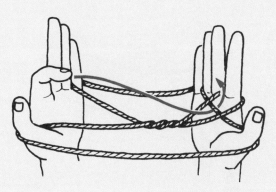

6 Your right thumb and right little finger drop their loops. Pull your right index finger out as far as it will go so that the loops move up the string towards your left hand. Now you've made the Fish Spear.

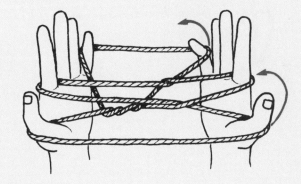

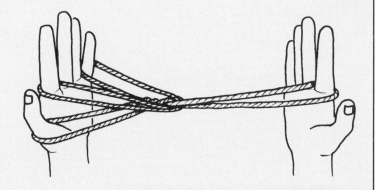

The Winking Eye

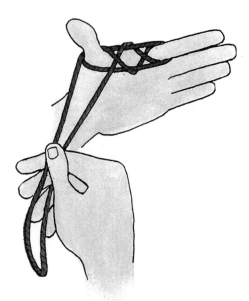

This string figure came from the Hawaiian island of Kauai. Use your imagination and you can really see the eye wink.

1 Hang the string loop over the fingers (but not the thumb) of your left hand.

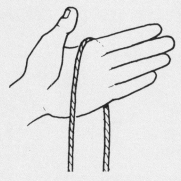

2 Your left middle, ring and little fingers close on the string hanging down across the palm of your hand. Your index finger still points out.

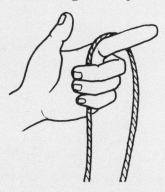

3 Your right index finger and thumb take the back string of the hanging loop, wrap it all the way around your left index finger, then bring it forward to hang up on your thumb.

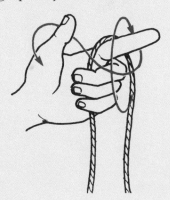

4 Your right index finger and thumb pull out the loop around your left index finger to share it with your left thumb. Be careful not to twist the loop when you do this.

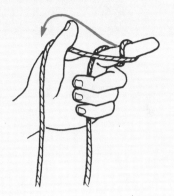

5 Take the string of the hanging loop that is nearest to you, lift it up over the string that runs between your index finger and thumb, and let it hang down in front of this string between your index finger and thumb.

6 Take the other string of the hanging loop (the one you have been holding) and lift it up to hang over your thumb.

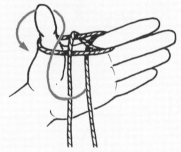

HOW TO MAKE THE EYE WINK

7 To close the eye, pull sideways on the strings of the hanging loop, and let your left index finger and thumb come closer together.

8 To open the eye, pull your left index finger and thumb farther apart and loosen your hold on the strings of the hanging loop.

The Siberian House

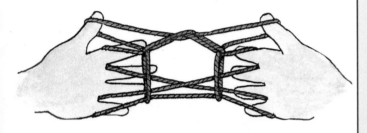

This Inuit figure is a little more difficult than the first two figures, but it's worth the effort. Hold on to the house once you've made it, because the next step shows the house breaking and the two people running away in opposite directions.

1 Do Opening A.

2 Turn your hands so that your palms are facing you, and put all your fingers down into the thumb loops.

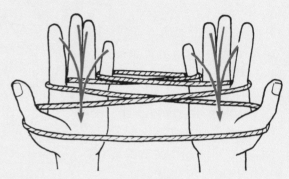

3 Throw the thumb loops over the backs of your hands and return your hands to the basic position. Be sure to keep all the loops separate. The loops around the backs of your hands should be lower than the index loops.

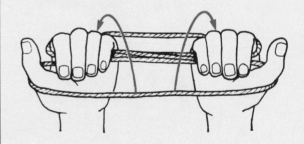

4 Your thumbs hook down the strings that go around the backs of your hands (the near strings of the hand loops) and go under all the other strings to pick up, from below, the far string of the hand loop. Return under the strings of the index loops. You now have a loop on each thumb.

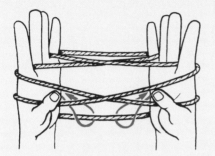 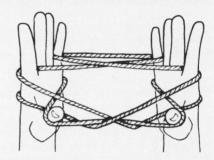

5 With your right thumb and index finger, take hold of the string that goes around the back of your left hand and lift it up over your fingers (but not over your thumb) to lie on the palm side of your left hand.

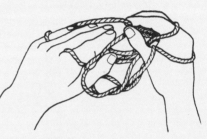

*Be careful not to lose any of the loops on your right fingers as you do this.

6 With your left thumb and index finger, take hold of the string that goes around the back of your right hand and lift it up over your fingers (but not your thumb) to lie on the palm side of your right hand.

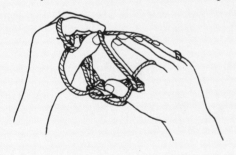 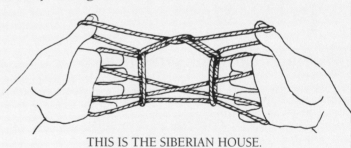

THIS IS THE SIBERIAN HOUSE.

7 When you release the loops from your index fingers and pull out gently with your hands, you can see two people running away in opposite directions.

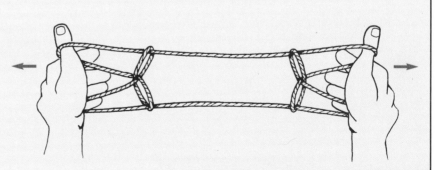

The Yam Thief

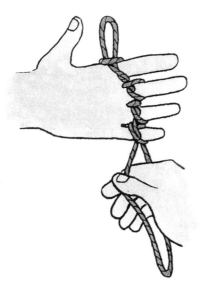

The Inuit called this string figure the Mouse and squeaked as they pulled the string off the fingers. In South America, it represented a snake crawling in and out of the trees. It also illustrated the tale of some stolen yams.

1 Hang the string loop over the fingers and thumb of your left hand.

2 Put your right hand into the hanging loop so that both hands are facing in the same direction. Use your right index finger like a hook to take hold of the string that crosses the space between your left thumb and index finger.

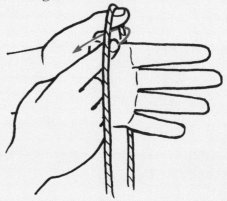

3 Now, with your right index finger, pull out a short loop in this string. Pull the loop out under the string that hangs over your left thumb. You must keep this loop straight.

4 Hold this loop with your right index finger and thumb and give it half a twist clockwise (make an X in it towards your left little finger).

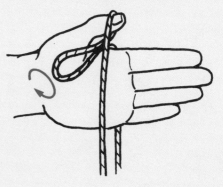

5 Put this loop on your left index finger, and pull on the hanging loop to tighten the strings. Be careful not to twist the loop again when you put it on your finger.

Now you repeat this to put loops on the rest of your fingers. Keep one string hanging down across your palm and one hanging down the back of your hand. Always put your right index finger under the string hanging down across your palm and use it like a hook.

6 Pull out a loop, in the back string, between your index finger and middle finger. Make sure you pull it out under the string that hangs across your palm. Give it half a twist ⌒➤ clockwise and put it on your middle finger. Tighten the strings.

7 Pull out a loop between your middle finger and ring finger, give it half a twist ⌒➤ clockwise and put it on your ring finger. Tighten the strings.

8 Pull out a loop between your ring finger and little finger, give it half a twist ⌒➤ clockwise and put it on your little finger. Tighten the strings.

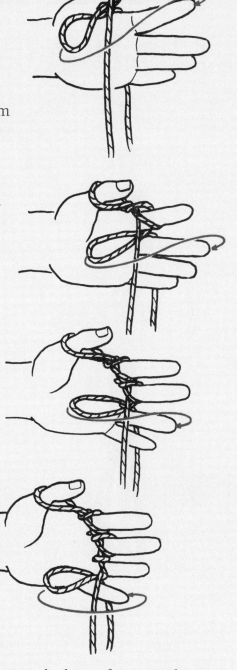

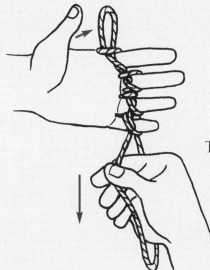

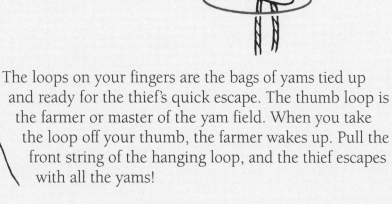

The loops on your fingers are the bags of yams tied up and ready for the thief's quick escape. The thumb loop is the farmer or master of the yam field. When you take the loop off your thumb, the farmer wakes up. Pull the front string of the hanging loop, and the thief escapes with all the yams!

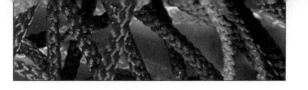

The Hogan and the Bunch of Bananas

This figure represents a Navaho tent, which is called a Hogan. It also makes a bunch of bananas. Are you hungry?

1 Hang the string loop around the back of the index and middle fingers of your left hand. The long loop hangs down across your palm.

2 Your right index finger goes into the hanging loop from behind, then between your left index and middle fingers. Use this finger like a hook to take hold of the string that goes behind your left index and middle fingers.

Pull this loop out as far as it will go, letting the string loop slide off your wrist. Let go of the string.

3 Your right hand goes into the long hanging loop from below. Your right thumb and index finger take hold of the strings that go between your left index and middle fingers. Make sure that you pick them up above the single front loop.

4 Pull out these strings as far as they will go, letting the wrist loop slide off your right hand as you pull. Keep holding the loop with your right thumb and index finger. Be careful not to twist the loop.

Now make this loop wider by putting the rest of the fingers of your right hand into the loop.

*This double string loop has two top strings (the strings that run between your left index and middle fingers) and two bottom strings.

5 Your left thumb and little finger each take, from below, one of the bottom strings. Drop the strings held by your right hand.

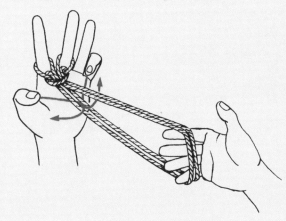

6 There is a small loop that goes around the loops on your left index and middle fingers. With your right thumb and index finger, gently pull out this small loop. Don't pull too far or the figure will fall apart.

7 This is the Navaho Hogan.

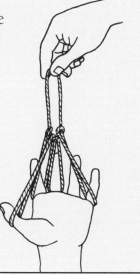

8 When you take the fingers of your left hand out of their loops, you have the Bunch of Bananas. See if your friends can pick one banana without taking the whole bunch.

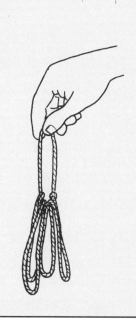

The Ghost Dance

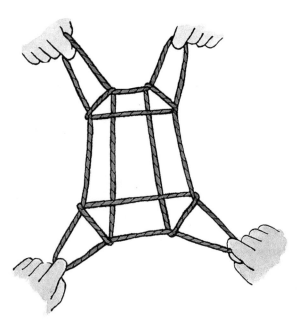

It takes two people and two strings to make this dancing ghost from Papua New Guinea. You can make it grow skinny or fat, hop, jump or dance on one leg. The fun can go on until someone stamps on the floor and shouts to frighten the ghost, which then collapses into a pile of loose strings.

Are you ready? The people are named A and B; the strings are numbered 1 and 2.

1 A and B hang string loop 1 around their necks. They sit or stand far enough apart so that the strings of the loop are tight.

2 A and B put their hands, from below, up into string loop 2. The loop lies over their wrists. They bend their wrists so that their fingers are pointing up and their palms are facing away from them. String loop 2 now has wrist strings and side strings and is roughly square.

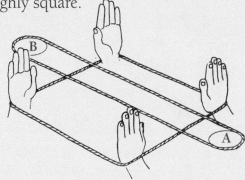

3 A's left index finger and thumb tip down to pick up A's left side string. A's right index finger and thumb tip down to pick up A's right side string.

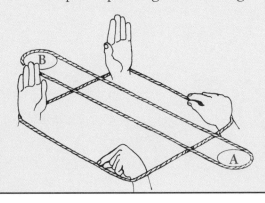

4 B does the same, so B's left index finger and thumb take B's left side string, and B's right index finger and thumb take B's right side string.

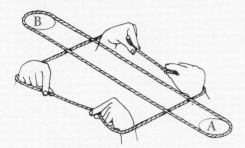

5 A's left and right hand want to exchange strings. So do B's. Be careful to keep the wrist loops as you do this. A's left hand and B's right hand, carrying their string, move towards the center of the figure to meet A's right hand and B's left hand carrying their string. One side string will cross over, one under the other as the strings change hands.

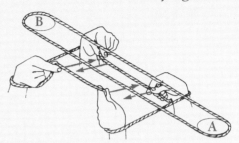

6 Now A and B let the wrist loops slide off their wrists and off their hands to lie over the crossed strings of loop 2.

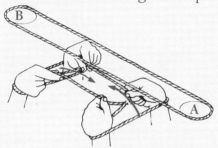

7 A and B are each holding two loops with their thumbs and index fingers. These loops now become index loops as A and B put their index fingers only up into them from below.

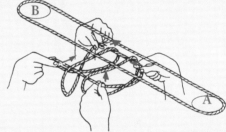

8 A and B raise string loop 2 until it rests just below string loop 1. Their index fingers hook down over string loop 1 and pull string loop 1 out through the old index loops. Don't worry about the old index loops — they will just slip off your index fingers.

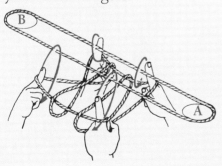

9 A and B take their heads out of string loop 1 and pull gently on the loops they are holding. You've made the ghost! Put the ghost's feet on the ground, make it stand up straight, and the ghost is ready to dance.

To make the ghost short and fat, A and B pull their hands apart. To make it tall and skinny, they bring their hands close together. Remember to keep the strings extended all the time. Now have fun making ghost noises — until someone shouts "Boo!"

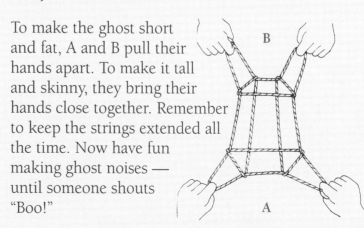

The Lizard

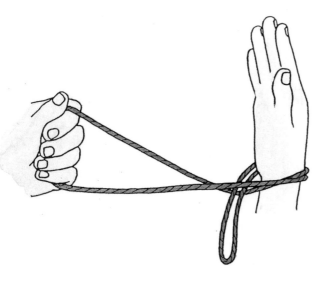

The Lizard is a string trick that was first collected from the Torres Straits in the South Pacific. When you've learned it, you can dazzle your friends by doing it several times in a row. In the Loyalty Islands, this slippery string trick was used when it was time to stop playing with string.

1 Hold the string loop with your left hand. Let the long loop hang down freely. The loop has a near side (close to you) and a far side (far from you on the other side of the strings).

2 Hold your right hand palm down with the fingers facing away from you, and put your hand through the string loop from the near side.

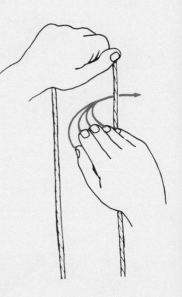

3 Tilt your right hand until the thumb faces down and then bend your wrist until your fingers are facing towards the right. The right hanging string is caught in the crook of your wrist.

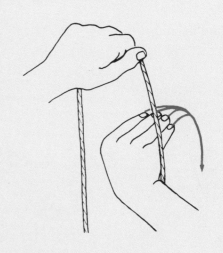

4 Catch this string (the right hanging string) on the back of your right thumb, then let this string slide over the rest of the fingers of your right hand until it is looped around your right wrist. Your right hand rotates as you do this, the fingers facing down, then towards the left. Your palm is facing in.

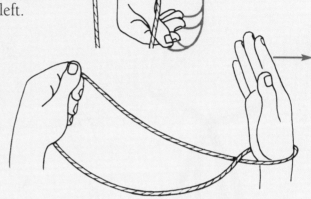

5 Continue to rotate your right hand until your fingers are facing up. Now turn your hand so that the palm is facing out, away from you. The right string of the hanging loop is still around your wrist.

6 Move your right hand, palm out, across the front of the figure to the left of the left string of the hanging loop, then away from you to the far side of the string loop.

7 Move your hand, still palm out, a little to the right, until it is behind the hanging loop. Your right hand has taken the right string of the hanging loop with it. This right string crosses over the left string, creating an upper space framed by the strings of the loop.

8 Bring your right hand, back first, towards you between the strings of this small upper space.

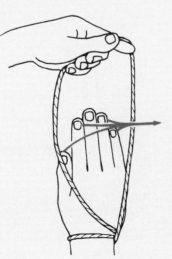

9 As you pull away the long loop with your left hand, the strings will slither off your right wrist.

Now do it again!

The Fly

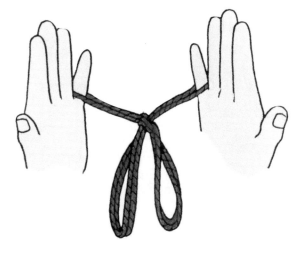

This version of the Fly comes from the Solomon Islands, which are near Papua New Guinea, in the Pacific Ocean. It was also known as a mosquito, a locust and even a flying fox.

You clap your hands together to try and catch that fly, but when you pull your hands apart, you'll find the fly has escaped again. Maybe your friends will have better luck!

1 Hang the string loop on your little fingers.

2 Your thumbs get both strings of the little finger loops.

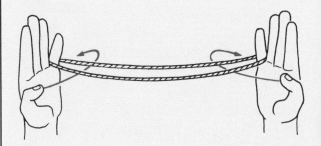

3 Your right index finger gets the two left palmar strings.

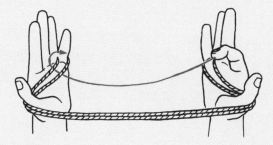

4 Your left thumb goes over the far index strings to pick up, from below, the two right palmar strings, not between, but beside, the strings of the right index loop.

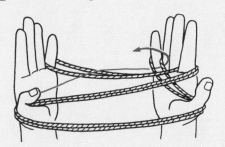

5 Navaho the left thumb loops.

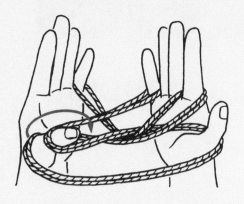

6 Your right thumb drops its loops. Now, pull the strings tight.

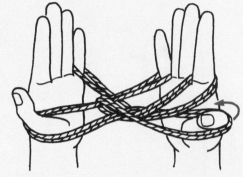

7 Your left thumb and right index finger drop their loops to release the fly's wings. Don't pull with your little fingers yet.

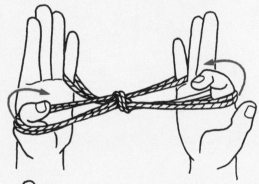

8 You clap your hands to catch the fly.

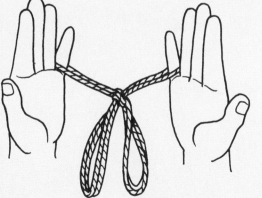

9 Your little fingers now pull out their loops to show that the fly is gone.

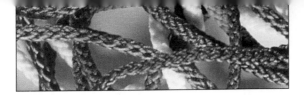

Man Climbing a Tree

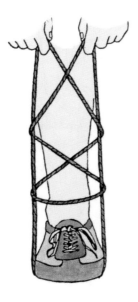

Someone looked at a drawing of this completed figure and worked backwards through all the steps to re-create the man climbing the tree. This is one string puzzle that was solved! Man Climbing a Tree is originally from Australia. You will see that the higher the man climbs, the smaller he gets.

1 Do Opening A.

2 Turn your hands so that your palms are facing you.

3 Your little fingers go over all the strings to get the near thumb string and then return.

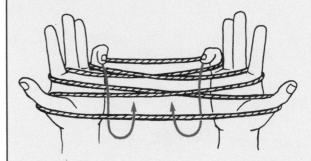

4 Each little finger now has two loops. You want to Navaho these loops. Make sure that the new far little finger string (the one you just picked up from your thumbs) stays above the old far little finger string.

Your right index finger and thumb pick up the lower far little finger string near your left little finger, carry it over the top of your left little finger, and let it lie in the center of the figure.

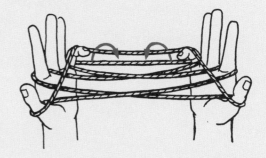

Your left index finger and thumb pick up the lower far little finger string near your right little finger, carry it over the top of your right little finger, and let it lie in the center of the figure.

The loops you have just Navahoed must stay on the far side of the index loops.

5 There is a palmar string that crosses each index loop. Hook your index fingers over these strings and down into the index loops.

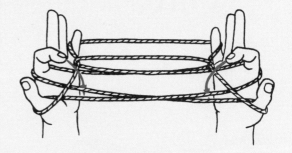

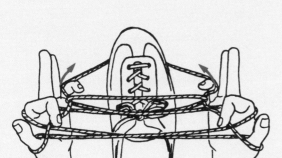

6 Put your foot into the big loop held by your little fingers, and take your little fingers out.

7 Now drop the loops from your thumbs. Each thumb can push off the opposite thumb loop, but hold on tightly to the strings under your index fingers as you do this. The loops on your index fingers will slip off by themselves.

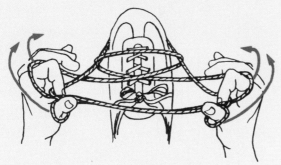

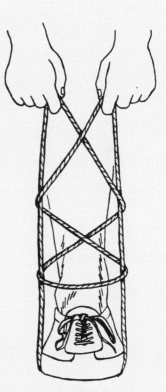

8 Pull gently with your index fingers and you will see the man with his arms and legs wrapped around the tree.

9 To make him climb the tree, pull gently with your right index finger, then with your left. As you keep doing this, he will climb higher and higher.

Open the Gate

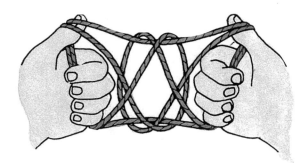

In Hawaii, this figure is called Open the Gate. In Fiji, it shows a point of land and an island that are sadly separated, even when the tide goes out. And in Papua New Guinea, two birds fly away from each other calling "Kokoko."

1 Do Opening A.

2 Your thumbs go over the strings of the index loops to get the near little finger strings and return.

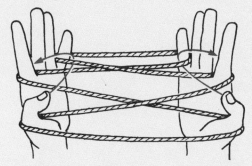

3 Your little fingers, without losing their loops, go over the strings of the index loops to get the far thumb strings and return.

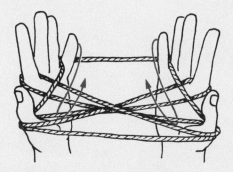

4 Your index fingers hook over the double palmar strings and go down into the index loops. Hold these palmar strings tightly under your index fingers to keep the strings steady.

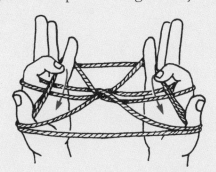

5 Your little fingers drop their loops.

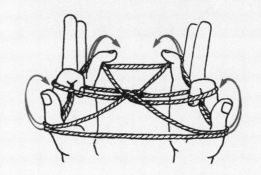

6 Your thumbs drop their loops.

7 Still holding on tightly with your index fingers, let the old index loops slide off your index fingers. Don't pull your hands apart to let the palmar strings slide yet.

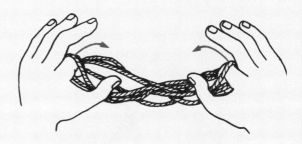

8 Put your middle, ring and little fingers into the index loops.

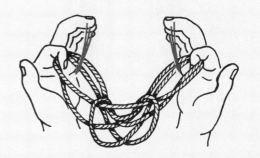

9 Now make the gate taller by using your thumbs to lift up the top strings of the loops held by your fingers.

10 As you pull your hands apart and let the double strings around your thumbs and under your fingers slide, the gate will open.

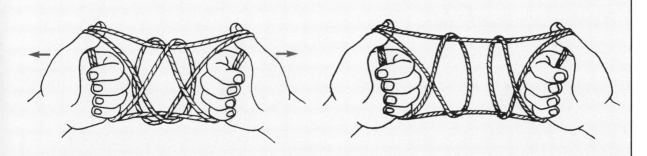

The Leashing of Lochiel's Dogs

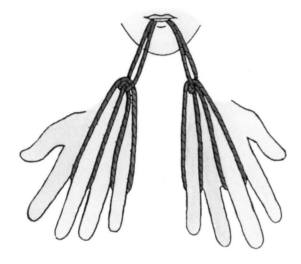

This figure was collected in Scotland, but it's found in many other parts of the world and has many names: Ptarmigan's Feet, or Crow's Feet, in North America; Chicken Toes, or the Wooden Spoon, in Africa; and the Spade in New Zealand. It's a type of catch, where strings are caught part way down the figure when loops are dropped.

1 Do Opening A.

2 Turn your hands so that the palms are facing you, and put all your fingers down into the thumb loops.

3 Throw the thumb loops over the backs of your hands and return your hands to the basic position. The loops around the backs of your hands should be lower than the index and little finger loops.

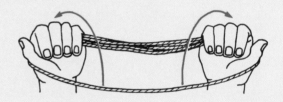

4 To transfer the index loops to your thumbs, your thumbs go up into the index loops. Now take your index fingers out of their loops.

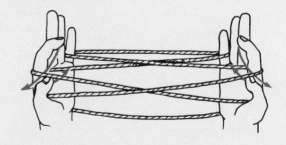

5 Your right index finger and thumb lift the loop off the back of your left hand and put it on your left middle finger.

6 Your left index finger and thumb lift the loop off the back of your right hand and put it on your right middle finger.

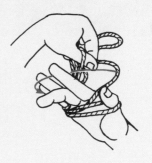

7 Your little fingers hook down over the far middle finger string and move it out of the way into the middle of the little finger loops. Now your little fingers can go down into the little finger loops to get the near little finger strings and straighten up.

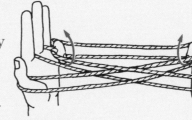

8 Each little finger now has two loops. To Navaho these loops, your right index finger and thumb pick up the lower far little finger string near your left little finger, carry it over the top of your left little finger, and let it lie on the near side of your little finger.

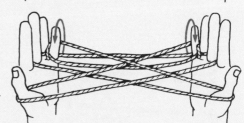

Your left index finger and thumb pick up the lower far little finger string near your right little finger, carry it over the top of your right little finger, and let it lie on the near side of your right little finger. Return your hands to the basic position.

The loops that you've Navahoed make one straight string that runs across the figure.

9 Your thumbs drop their loops. Now pull the strings until they are tight to make the dogs on their leashes.

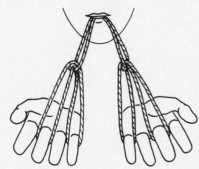

10 To make Crow's Feet, you pick up the double strings in the middle of the figure with your teeth, and you bring your hands close together, palms up.

Cameron of Lochiel was a seventeenth-century Scottish Highland chieftain who was famous for his feats of strength and his fierceness in battle.

A Bird

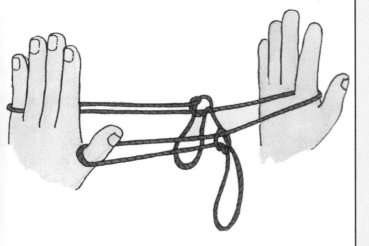

This bird comes from Papua New Guinea. You can make him fly across the string — but only in one direction!

1 Do Position 1 on your left hand.

2 With your right index finger and thumb, pull out the left palmar string as far as it will go.

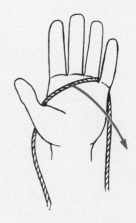

3 With your right index finger and thumb, pull out the new left palmar string as far as it will go.

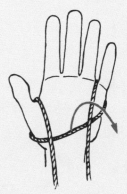

4 Put your right thumb and little finger, from the front, into the hanging loop.

5 From the outside, put your right thumb into the left thumb loop and, also from the outside, put your right little finger into the left little finger loop.

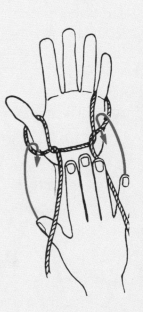

6 Use your thumb and little finger like hooks to pull these loops out as far as they will go. You have made a string triangle near your left hand.

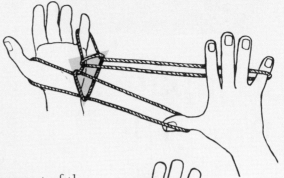

7 Take your right thumb and little finger out of the loops they are holding. From the front, near the string triangle, put your right thumb into the hanging thumb loop and your right little finger into the hanging little finger loop.

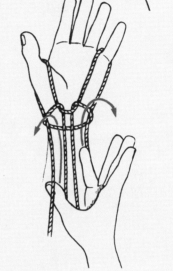

8 Put these fingers up behind the string that makes the base of the string triangle.

9 Gently draw this string out as far as it will go. Now there is a string diamond near your right hand. (If you pull too hard, the diamond, and the bird, will be too small.)

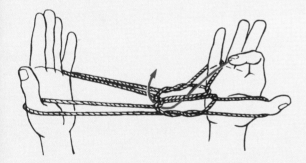

10 There is a loop that runs out from between your left little finger and ring finger, down to the diamond and back between your left index finger and thumb. With your left index finger and thumb, pick up this loop inside the diamond and put it on your right index finger.

See-saw your hands away from each other to tighten the strings a little.

11 Drop the loops from your right thumb and little finger (these loops are the wings), and pull with your right index finger to make the bird fly along the string.

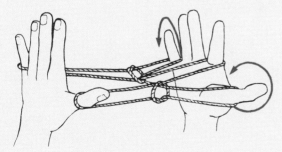

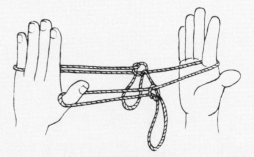

The Japanese Butterfly

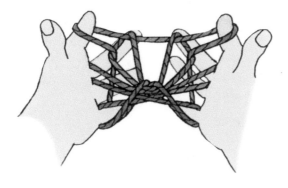

There are many Japanese string figures of dragonflies and butterflies. String artist Bill Russell learned this one from a Japanese-Canadian schoolgirl. It's not too hard, and it's very beautiful.

1 Hang the string loop on your thumbs.

2 Your left little finger picks up, from below, the left far thumb string to put the string loop in Position 1 on your left hand.

3 Bend down your right index, middle and ring fingers, but leave your little finger standing tall to make the next move easier. Now your right little finger dives, from the top, down behind the left palmar string.

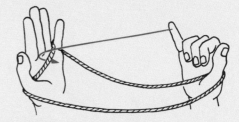

4 Turn your right little finger away from you and up, and return all your fingers to the basic position.

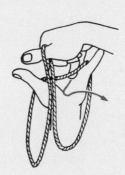

Both thumbs and little fingers have loops on them, and there is a cross in the middle of the figure. Make sure that the near little finger string is one straight string running from hand to hand.

5 Your index fingers tip down and go up into the little finger loops to get the near little finger string and return.

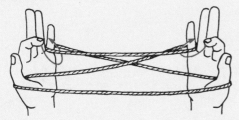

6 Now do Opening A with your middle fingers, picking up the loops that cross in front of your middle and ring fingers.

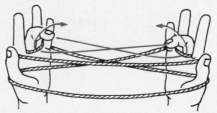

7 Turn your hands so that the palms are facing you. Your little fingers move over the strings to get the far thumb strings. Return your hands to the basic position.

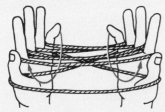

8 Your index fingers hook over the palmar strings (the strings that run across the loops from thumbs to little fingers) and down into the index loops.

9 Your index fingers still hang on to these palmar strings while your thumbs release their loops.

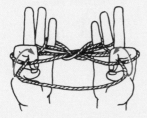

10 Now turn your hands again so that the palms are facing you, and let the old index loops slide off your index fingers.

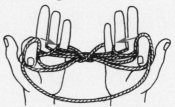

11 Your index fingers straighten up. The strings under your index fingers become the new index loops.

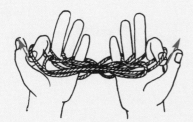

12 Return your hands to the basic position. Now turn your hands so that your fingers are pointing away from you to show off the Butterfly.

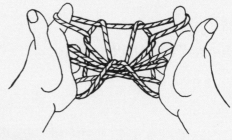

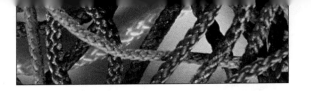

The Fishnet

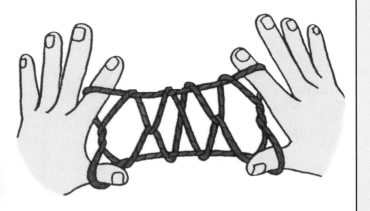

The figure of the Fishnet appeared in many parts of the world. It has also been called Osage Diamonds and Jacob's Ladder. In Africa, it was called a Calabash Net — a net used for carrying a large gourd. And in Quebec, it's le pont de Québec, the Quebec Bridge.

1 Do Opening A.

2 Your thumbs drop their loops.

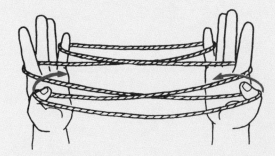

3 Turn your hands away from you with the palms facing out and the thumbs facing down.

4 Your thumbs pick up from below the far little finger string (the bottom string) and return under the strings of the index loops.

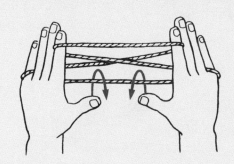

5 Your thumbs go over the near index string to get the far index strings and return.

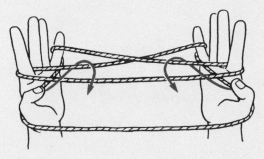

6 Your little fingers drop their loops.

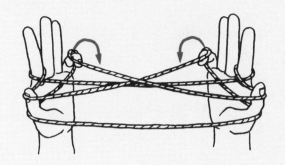

7 Your little fingers go over the near index strings to get the far thumb strings and return.

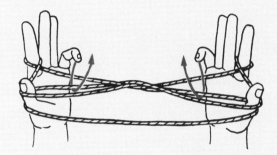

8 Your thumbs drop their loops. This is Cat's Whiskers. You can meow if you like!

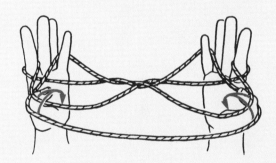

9 Your thumbs go over both strings of the index loops to get the near little finger strings and return.

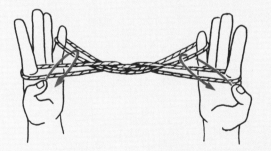

Keep going …

10 Use your right thumb and index finger to pull out the left index loop and share it with your left thumb.

11 Do this again to share the right index loop with your right thumb.

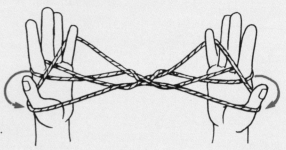

12 Tip your thumbs down (or use your fingers or teeth) to Navaho first the left thumb loops, then the right.

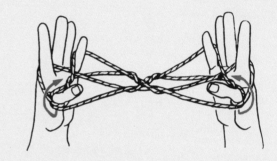

13 Near each thumb there is a string triangle. Your index fingers go down into these triangles.

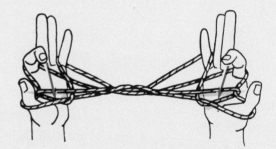

14 Gently take your little fingers out of their loops.

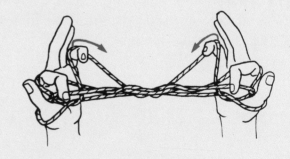

15 Turn your hands so that the palms face away from you. Don't worry about the index loops. They will just slip off your index fingers.

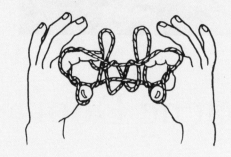

16 Your index fingers straighten up to extend the Fishnet.

To avoid squashed diamonds:
Don't pull your hands apart; just stretch your index fingers and thumbs as you extend the net.

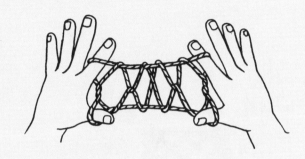

17 To make the Eiffel Tower, pick up the top string of the net between the two middle diamonds with your teeth and pull. Keep hanging on to that string with your teeth. Now you can go on to make the Witch's Hat.

18 To make the Witch's Hat, pick up the top string of the net between the two middle diamonds. Your index fingers drop their loops and you pull down with your thumbs.

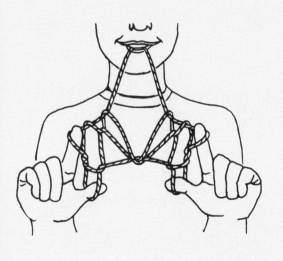

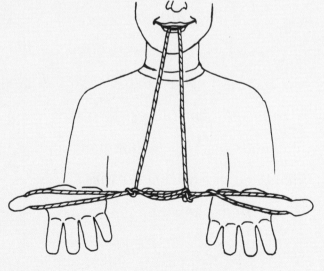

Apache Door

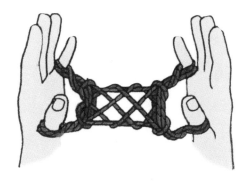

This figure shows the decorated door flap of an Apache tent. It is longer and more difficult than many of the other figures in this book, but the finished pattern is very beautiful. Don't forget to rub your hands together to summon the magic that will make the figure appear.

1 Do Position 1.

2 Put your whole right hand under the left palmar string and, as you pull it out, let the string loop slide down around your right wrist.

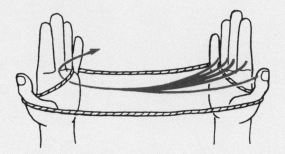

3 Put your whole left hand, thumb too, under the right palmar string and, as you pull it out, let the string loop slide down around your left wrist.

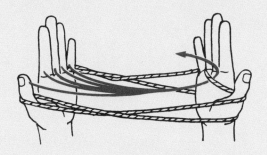

4 Your thumbs get the near little finger strings and return.

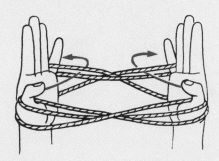

5 Your little fingers get the far thumb strings and return.

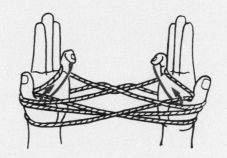

6 With your whole right hand, take hold of all the strings in the middle of the figure.

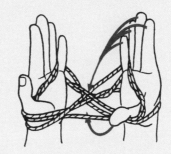

7 Put all these strings between your left index finger and thumb. Make sure these strings don't cover up the thumb loops — you'll need these. Then let go of the strings you are holding with your right hand.

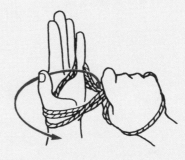

8 Now, use your right index finger and thumb to take hold of the two left thumb loops and hang on to them. Don't move this right hand at all.

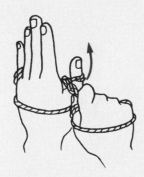

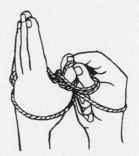

Keep going …

9 Take your left thumb out of these two thumb loops and out of the strings you have just wrapped around it.

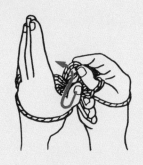

10 From below, slide your left thumb back into the two loops that your right index finger and thumb have been holding.

11 Repeat this for your right hand. So, with your left hand, take hold of all the strings in the middle of the figure.

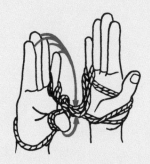

12 Put all these strings between your right index finger and thumb.

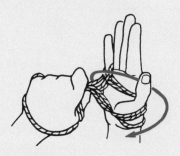

13 With your left index finger and thumb, take hold of the two right thumb loops and hang on to them. Remember not to move your left hand.

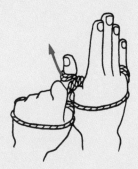

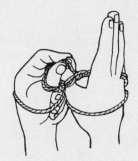

14 Take your right thumb out of these two thumb loops and out of the strings you have just wrapped around it.

15 From below, slide your right thumb back into the loops held by your left index finger and thumb.

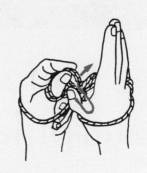

16 With your right index finger and thumb, take the left wrist loop off your left hand and let it lie in the middle of the figure.

17 With your left index finger and thumb, take the right wrist loop off your right hand and let it lie in the middle of the figure.

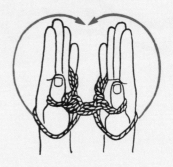

*Now comes the most important part. Put your hands together and rub the strings to summon the magic you will need to make the figure appear.

18 Extend the figure by pulling your hands apart. For best results, see-saw your hands up and down a little as you do this.

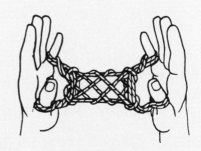

The Looper Caterpillar

This delightful moving figure from the South Pacific has many names. In New Caledonia, it's called the Looper Caterpillar. You can see why as you make it loop along. In the Solomon Islands, it's known as Worm Creeping. The Nauruans named it the Dancer, and in the Caroline Islands it's One Chief. An easy way of making it was collected in Papua New Guinea. There it's called Zissoci (Scissors?), and you are supposed to put the figure up to someone's head and pretend to cut the hair.

1 Do Position 1.

2 Your right thumb and index finger take the near left thumb string and wrap it once around your left thumb.

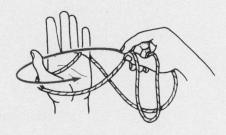

3 Your right index fingers goes, from below, up into this new little left thumb loop and returns.

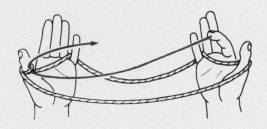

4 Your left index finger gets the right palmar string, as in Opening A, and returns.

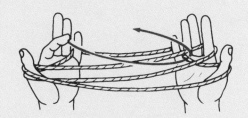

5 Your right index finger gets the left palmar string, as in Opening A, and returns. Your right index finger now has two loops — an upper loop and a lower loop. Be sure to keep them apart and don't let them get mixed up.

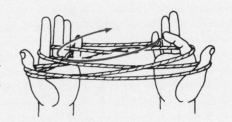

6 Turn your hands so that your right palm is facing down and the fingers of your right hand are pointing to the left.

7 Your left hand drops all its loops.

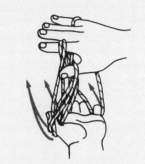

8 Your left thumb and little finger go into the upper right index loop. They take this loop off your right index finger. The string is in Position 1 on your left hand and your left hand is now in the basic position. Don't return your right hand to the basic position yet.

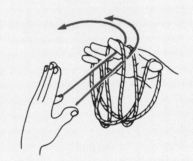

9 Put your left thumb and your right index finger tip to tip. Now slide the remaining right index loop onto your left thumb and return your hands to the basic position.

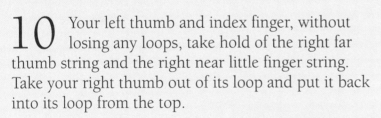

10 Your left thumb and index finger, without losing any loops, take hold of the right far thumb string and the right near little finger string. Take your right thumb out of its loop and put it back into its loop from the top.

11 Your right thumb also goes, from below, up into the right little finger loop and returns carrying the near little finger string as well as its own loop. Your left index finger and thumb drop the strings they are holding and return to the basic position.

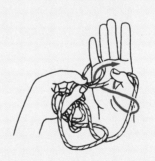

Keep going …

The figure is extended using the Caroline Extension:

12 Turn your hands until the palms are facing up. Your index fingers tip down over the palmar strings to go, from below, up into the thumb loops. They get the far thumb strings and return. Keep these strings high up on your index fingers.

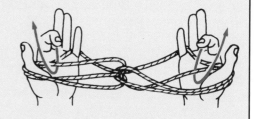

13 Your thumbs press against the strings that run from your index fingers down to your thumbs. Keep each index finger and thumb, with the string between them, pressed tightly together. Don't let this string move at all.

14 To extend the Caterpillar, turn your hands so that the palms are facing out. Curl your middle, ring and little fingers down over the far little finger string. This is comfortable and helps to steady the bottom framing string as the Caterpillar walks along.

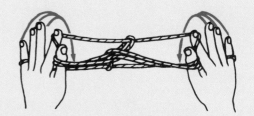

To make the Caterpillar walk, you alternately extend and collapse the figure.

To collapse the figure, rotate your hands until the palms are facing each other.

To extend the figure again, rotate your hands until the palms are facing out.

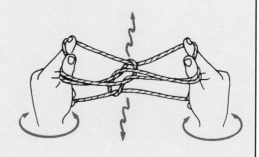

Now your Caterpillar can crawl along your lap or up somebody's arm.